THE POWER OF ENTREPRENEURIAL CONFIDENCE

BUILDING A BUSINESS EMPIRE

FATEMA ABBAS TINWALA

Made with ♥ on the Notion Press Platform
www.notionpress.com

Contents

Foreword

You have a strong backing in the form of your family business. Why worry?
You are a bright student. Try a profession like medicine because you can do it.

Brought up in a Gujarati-speaking household, I belong to a sub-community of Muslims that is widely recognised for its business mindset. This did not stop relatives from deciding my fate even before I knew that after attempting your 10th board, life isn't a cakewalk. I have come across two types of people while figuring out my career

1. Those who felt I had an edge over the rest because of my family business and the business mindset I possess.
2. Those who felt I could crack difficult exams and become a doctor or a CA because I was intelligent.

It was after a lot of permutation, combinations, introspection and messy phases, that I realised my true calling in training & coaching. From attempting it as a live project to turning it into a startup, the relatives in the 1st category eventually won.

Competing in a fragmented market helped me realize that doing this out of passion will not pay my bills. This is when I started connecting with individuals from the industry who have walked my path; to learn the right methods and establish meaningful connections that can be nurtured in the long term.

A phase of networking spree brought me in touch with Fatema. Apart from our language and a knack for exchanging festive pleasantries, we connected on communication and confidence-building. Her insights on conflict management have always fascinated me from both theoretical and a practical point of view.

It could've been easy for a trainer who is involved with a well-reputed healthcare brand to enjoy the fruits of her hard work and pursue training as a passion. But,her growth is not restricted by this mindset. More than simply looking for new projects, she has proactively explored new learning resources and avenues for herself. She sees her career as an opportunity to work on her skills and evolve as a learner before giving her best as a trainer.

This book, ***"The Power of Entrepreneurial Confidence Building: A Business Empire"*** is a reflection of Fatema's personality. She profoundly discusses the core confidence-building areas; easing the pressure on the shoulders of aspiring entrepreneurs. It lets you explore your weaknesses to understand the gaps in executing your ideas. From analysing your fears to mentoring the right individuals to take your legacy forward, you can treat this book as a one-stop solution to constantly enrich your leadership skill; 90 days at a time

Nobody better than a trainer, who has not only walked that path while building her brand but also trained leaders in confidence-building, could have explain this to you effectively.

My heartfelt gratitude to Fatema for keeping the learning bug alive within and inspiring more entrepreneurs to strengthen their foundation. The more you run away from problems, the more they pile up. So, why not face them with confidence and deal with it? Nobody will believe in you if you don't believe in yourself. Consider this book as a reminder to do that.

Huzefa Hakim
Founder of Talk2Grow
Communication Coach & Life Skills Trainer

Preface

In the world of entrepreneurship, confidence is more than a trait; it's a superpower that fuels every step of the journey. The Power of Entrepreneurial Confidence was written for those who aspire to build not just businesses but empires fueled by resilience, innovation, and an unwavering belief in oneself.

When I began my own path in business, I often heard that confidence was a natural gift, something you either had or didn't. But experience soon taught me that confidence is a skill—a skill that anyone can cultivate, nurture, and grow, just like any other aspect of a successful business. The chapters that follow are designed to demystify confidence, offering practical tools and strategies to help you develop this skill as a foundation for your entrepreneurial ambitions.

This book takes you through each essential stage of building confidence. From overcoming self-doubt and embracing a growth mindset to leading with assurance and establishing strong relationships, you'll find methods to strengthen your personal and professional brand. You'll learn how to negotiate with conviction, network with authenticity, and inspire others around you. The goal is for you to walk away with actionable steps, empowering you to take risks, learn from failures, and continually adapt in a fast-changing business world.

I've filled these pages with insights, strategies, and exercises that have supported countless entrepreneurs and leaders in realizing their visions. These lessons don't just stop at individual growth—they also extend to building and sustaining a confident, collaborative team. After all, your confidence as a leader will often set the tone for your business, inspiring others to trust, innovate, and commit to a shared vision.

To every aspiring and established entrepreneur reading this: remember, your confidence will be your most valuable resource. Nurture it, believe in it, and use it to navigate the challenges and triumphs of building your empire. May this book serve as a guide, a companion, and a reminder that within you lies the power to achieve greatness.

Here's to your journey and the empire that awaits!

Fatema Abbas Tinwala
Corporate Psychologist

CHAPTER ONE

The Importance of Confidence in Entrepreneurship

Understanding the Role of Confidence in Business Success

Confidence is an essential quality that can greatly impact an entrepreneur's journey towards building a successful business empire. It serves as the driving force behind every decision, action, and interaction we make in the business world. In this subchapter, we delve into the power of confidence in entrepreneurship and how it can propel us to achieve remarkable success.

Confidence is not just a mere belief in oneself; it is a mindset that shapes our behavior, resilience, and determination. When entrepreneurs possess unwavering confidence in their abilities, they are more likely to take calculated risks, embrace challenges, and persevere in the face of adversity. This unwavering self-assuredness allows them to overcome obstacles and setbacks with a positive attitude, ensuring they stay focused on their goals.

One of the key aspects of confidence in entrepreneurship is the ability to inspire and lead others. When entrepreneurs exude confidence, they attract like-minded individuals who believe in their vision and are willing to work tirelessly towards its realization. Confidence acts as a magnet, attracting talented employees, investors, and partners who want to be a part of something extraordinary. It creates a positive and empowering work culture that enhances creativity, productivity, and collaboration within the organization.

Moreover, confidence enables entrepreneurs to effectively communicate and negotiate with stakeholders. Whether it's pitching a business idea to potential investors or negotiating a deal with suppliers, confidence is the key to winning over others and securing beneficial partnerships. It instills trust and credibility, making it easier to build strong professional relationships that are crucial for long-term success.

However, it is important to note that confidence should not be mistaken for arrogance or overconfidence. A confident entrepreneur knows their strengths and weaknesses, seeks continuous improvement, and is open to learning from others. They understand that confidence is not static, but rather a dynamic quality that requires constant nurturing and development.

In conclusion, understanding and harnessing the power of confidence is vital for entrepreneurs who aspire to build a business empire. It shapes not only our mindset but also our actions, influencing how we navigate challenges, attract valuable resources, and build strong relationships. By cultivating confidence, entrepreneurs can unlock their full potential and pave the way for unparalleled success in the dynamic and competitive world of business.

The Link Between Self-Confidence and Entrepreneurial Ventures

In the world of entrepreneurship, self-confidence is often cited as a crucial factor in determining the success of a venture. While many may associate entrepreneurship with risk-taking and innovation, it is the underlying belief in oneself that truly sets successful entrepreneurs apart. This subchapter will delve into the powerful connection between self-confidence and entrepreneurial ventures, exploring how a strong sense of self-assurance can propel individuals towards building a business empire.

To begin, it is important to understand the role of self-confidence in entrepreneurship. Entrepreneurs face numerous challenges and obstacles on their journey, from securing funding to making critical decisions. Without a firm belief in their abilities, entrepreneurs may be easily discouraged or hesitant to take the necessary risks. On the other hand, those with high levels of self-confidence are more likely to persevere, maintain a positive mindset, and seize opportunities when they arise.

One of the key benefits of self-confidence in entrepreneurship is the ability to inspire and lead others. Confidence is contagious, and when entrepreneurs exude self- assurance, it instills trust and belief in their team members, investors, and customers. This trust not only helps attract talented individuals to join the venture but also fosters a positive work environment conducive to creativity and innovation.

Moreover, self-confidence enables entrepreneurs to navigate challenges and setbacks more effectively. In the face of failure, confident individuals tend to view it as a temporary setback rather than a permanent defeat. They are more likely to bounce back, learn from their mistakes, and adapt their strategies accordingly. This resilience is a crucial trait in the entrepreneurial world, where setbacks are inevitable, and the ability to persevere is paramount.

Furthermore, self-confidence plays a significant role in attracting investors and securing funding. Investors look for entrepreneurs who exude confidence and conviction in their vision. A confident entrepreneur can effectively communicate their ideas, articulate the value proposition of their venture, and demonstrate their ability to execute their plans. This persuasive power is invaluable when seeking financial support for entrepreneurial endeavors.

In conclusion, self-confidence is intricately linked to the success of entrepreneurial ventures. Entrepreneurs who possess a strong sense of self-assurance are more likely to overcome challenges, inspire others, and attract the necessary resources to build a business empire. Developing and nurturing self-confidence should be a priority for all entrepreneurs, as it is the foundation upon which their entrepreneurial journey is built.

Overcoming Self-Doubt: Building a Strong Foundation for Success

In the journey of entrepreneurship, self-doubt can be the biggest obstacle standing between you and success. The power of confidence in entrepreneurship cannot be emphasized enough, as it forms the bedrock upon which your business empire can be built. In this subchapter, we will explore effective strategies to overcome self- doubt and forge a strong foundation for your entrepreneurial journey.

1. Acknowledge and Embrace Your Strengths:

Self-doubt often arises from a lack of self-awareness. Take the time to identify your unique strengths and talents. Understand what sets you apart from others in your niche. Embrace these qualities and believe in your ability to make a difference.

Confidence stems from self-acceptance and understanding your own worth.

2. Surround Yourself with a Supportive Network:

Building a strong support network is vital for overcoming self-doubt. Surround yourself with like-minded entrepreneurs who can provide mentorship, advice, and encouragement. Share your challenges and celebrate your victories with this network. Their belief in you will help strengthen your own belief in yourself.

3. Set Realistic Goals and Celebrate Milestones:

Breaking down your entrepreneurial journey into manageable goals is crucial for building confidence. Set realistic and achievable targets, both short-term and long- term. Celebrate every milestone you achieve, no matter how small. Recognizing your progress will help combat self-doubt and instill a sense of accomplishment.

4. Embrace Failure as a Stepping Stone:

Failure is an inevitable part of entrepreneurship, but it should never define you. Instead of allowing failures to fuel self-doubt, learn from them and use them as stepping stones towards success. Embrace the lessons, adjust your strategies, and keep moving forward. Every setback is an opportunity for growth and improvement.

5. Continuous Learning and Skill Development:

Investing in your personal and professional growth is crucial for building confidence. Stay up-to-date with industry trends, attend workshops, conferences, and seek out learning opportunities. Acquiring new skills and knowledge will not only enhance your expertise but also boost your confidence in tackling new challenges.

6. Practice Self-Care and Prioritize Mental Well-being:

Entrepreneurship can be demanding, both physically and mentally. It is essential to prioritize self-care and mental well-being. Take time for activities that rejuvenate you, such as exercise, meditation, or pursuing hobbies. Surround yourself with positivity and practice gratitude. A strong mind breeds confidence and resilience.

In conclusion, overcoming self-doubt is an ongoing journey that requires perseverance and self-belief. By acknowledging your strengths, building a supportive network, setting realistic goals, embracing failure, continuously learning, and practicing self-care, you can lay a strong foundation for success. Remember, confidence is the fuel that propels entrepreneurial ventures, and with it, you can truly build a business empire.

CHAPTER TWO

Cultivating Entrepreneurial Confidence

Developing a Growth Mindset: Embracing Challenges and Failures

In the realm of entrepreneurship, having a growth mindset is crucial for success. It is the foundation upon which great achievements are built. In this subchapter, we will explore the significance of embracing challenges and failures as essential components of developing a growth mindset.

Entrepreneurs often face numerous obstacles on their path to building a business empire, but those with a growth mindset view these challenges as opportunities for growth and learning. They understand that setbacks and failures are not roadblocks, but rather stepping stones towards success. Embracing challenges allows entrepreneurs to push their boundaries, develop new skills, and gain valuable experience.

Failure, despite its negative connotation, is an integral part of the entrepreneurial journey. Instead of fearing failure, entrepreneurs with a growth mindset embrace it as a necessary part of the learning process. They understand that failure provides valuable lessons and insights that can be applied to future endeavors. By reframing failures as valuable feedback, entrepreneurs can adapt, iterate, and improve their strategies, ultimately increasing their chances of success.

To develop a growth mindset, entrepreneurs need to shift their perspective on challenges and failures. Instead of viewing them as personal shortcomings, they should see them as opportunities for growth. By reframing challenges as exciting prospects to learn and develop, entrepreneurs can overcome any self-limiting beliefs and unlock their full potential.

Embracing challenges and failures also cultivates resilience, a vital trait for entrepreneurs. The ability to bounce back from setbacks and maintain a positive attitude in the face of adversity is what sets successful entrepreneurs apart. By continuously embracing challenges and failures, entrepreneurs strengthen their resilience, enabling them to navigate the ever-changing landscape of entrepreneurship with confidence and determination.

Additionally, embracing challenges and failures fosters an environment of innovation and creativity. Entrepreneurs who are unafraid to take risks, experiment, and learn from failures are more likely to develop groundbreaking ideas and solutions. These individuals are not discouraged by initial setbacks but rather motivated to find alternative approaches and unconventional paths to success.

In conclusion, developing a growth mindset is crucial for entrepreneurs aiming to build a business empire. Embracing challenges and failures as opportunities for growth and learning is what sets successful entrepreneurs apart. By shifting their perspective, reframing failures, and cultivating resilience, entrepreneurs can unlock their full potential and confidently navigate the entrepreneurial landscape.

Remember, challenges and failures are not roadblocks but stepping stones on the path to success.

Building a Personal Brand: Leveraging Confidence to Attract Opportunities

In the ever-evolving world of entrepreneurship, one thing remains constant – the power of confidence. As entrepreneurs, we are constantly faced with challenges, obstacles, and the need to prove ourselves. In this subchapter, we delve into the importance of building a personal brand and how leveraging confidence can attract incredible opportunities.

Your personal brand is your unique identity in the business world. It is how you present yourself to potential clients, partners, and investors. Building a strong personal brand is essential for establishing credibility, trust, and ultimately attracting opportunities that can propel your business empire forward.

Confidence is the key ingredient in developing a powerful personal brand. When you believe in yourself and your abilities, others naturally gravitate towards you.

Confidence exudes competence, authority, and leadership. People are more likely to trust and do business with someone who radiates confidence.

To build your personal brand, start by identifying your strengths, values, and unique selling points. What sets you apart from others in your niche? What can you bring to the table that no one else can? Once you have a clear understanding of your brand identity, use confidence to amplify that message.

Confidence is not something that can be faked. It comes from a deep-rooted belief in your abilities and a genuine passion for what you do. Embrace your expertise and showcase it in every interaction and opportunity. Speak up, share your knowledge, and be unapologetically yourself. Remember, confidence is contagious, and when people see your unwavering belief in yourself, they will be inspired to believe in you too.

Leveraging confidence to attract opportunities requires proactive networking and relationship-building. Attend industry events, join relevant communities, and engage with influential individuals in your niche. Approach these interactions with a sense of self-assuredness, knowing that you have something valuable to offer. As you build relationships based on trust and mutual respect, opportunities will naturally present themselves.

Furthermore, confidence is not just about how you present yourself externally. It also involves inner self-belief and resilience. As an entrepreneur, you will face setbacks, rejection, and moments of doubt. However, it is your unwavering confidence that will help you bounce back, learn from failures, and adapt to changing circumstances.

In conclusion, building a personal brand and leveraging confidence are crucial aspects of entrepreneurial success. Your personal brand is your unique identity, and confidence is the fuel that propels it forward. Believe in yourself, embrace your expertise, and actively seek out opportunities. With confidence as your ally, you will attract incredible opportunities that will contribute to building your business empire.

The Power of Positive Thinking: Harnessing Confidence for Success

In the realm of entrepreneurship, confidence is a superpower that can propel you towards success. It is the driving force that allows you to take risks, overcome challenges, and turn your dreams into reality. The power of positive thinking, combined with unwavering self-belief, can truly transform your entrepreneurial journey.

Confidence is not just a state of mind; it is an essential trait that sets successful entrepreneurs apart from the rest. When you have confidence in yourself and your abilities, you radiate an aura of conviction and determination. This aura attracts opportunities, investors, and collaborators, paving the way for your business empire to flourish.

Harnessing confidence begins with adopting a positive mindset. Instead of dwelling on failures or setbacks, successful entrepreneurs focus on solutions and opportunities. They understand that challenges are merely stepping stones towards growth and improvement. By training your mind to embrace positivity, you can overcome self-doubt and unleash your full potential.

One effective way to cultivate positivity is through affirmations and visualization. Repeat empowering statements like "I am capable of achieving greatness" or "I have the skills and knowledge to succeed" to reinforce your self-belief. Visualize yourself accomplishing your goals and experiencing the success you desire. This practice rewires your brain, reinforcing positive thoughts and replacing self-limiting beliefs with confidence.

Confidence also thrives when you surround yourself with a supportive network. Seek out mentors, like-minded entrepreneurs, and a community that uplifts and inspires you. When you are surrounded by individuals who believe in your vision and capabilities, it becomes easier to maintain a positive mindset and overcome obstacles.

Remember, confidence is not about being arrogant or reckless. It is about having faith in your abilities while acknowledging that there is always room for growth and learning. Successful entrepreneurs embrace failure as a valuable teacher and use it to refine their strategies and approach.

In conclusion, the power of positive thinking and harnessing confidence is undeniable in the world of entrepreneurship. By cultivating a positive mindset, visualizing success, and surrounding yourself with a supportive network, you can unlock your entrepreneurial potential and build a thriving business empire. Embrace the power of confidence, and watch your dreams unfold before your eyes.

CHAPTER THREE

Nurturing Confidence in Business Relationships

Networking with Confidence: Making Lasting Connections

In the fast-paced and competitive world of entrepreneurship, networking has become an essential skill for success. Building a strong network of professional connections can open doors, create opportunities, and propel your business forward. However, many entrepreneurs struggle with networking, feeling intimidated or unsure of how to make lasting connections. This subchapter, titled "Networking with Confidence: Making Lasting Connections," aims to address the power of confidence in entrepreneurship, specifically in the context of networking.

Confidence is the key to making a lasting impact on others and forging meaningful connections. When you exude confidence, people are naturally drawn to you, and doors that were once closed suddenly open. But confidence doesn't come naturally to everyone, and that's okay. In this subchapter, we will explore techniques and strategies to help entrepreneurs develop and project confidence while networking.

First and foremost, it's crucial to believe in yourself and your abilities. Entrepreneurship is inherently challenging, and self-doubt can be a constant companion. By reminding yourself of your achievements, unique skills, and the value you bring to the table, you can boost your self-confidence and approach networking with a positive mindset.

We will discuss the importance of setting clear networking goals and identifying target individuals or groups to connect with. Having a purpose and a plan will give you direction and focus, making networking more effective and less daunting.

Additionally, we will provide tips on how to approach networking events, engage in meaningful conversations, and leave a lasting impression.

Building authentic relationships is at the core of successful networking. We will delve into ways to establish genuine connections by being a good listener, showing empathy, and offering support to others. By cultivating meaningful relationships, you can create a network of individuals who genuinely believe in your vision and are willing to support you along your entrepreneurial journey.

Lastly, we will discuss the importance of maintaining and nurturing your network. Networking is not a one-time event but an ongoing process. We will explore strategies for staying connected with your contacts, nurturing relationships, and leveraging your network to benefit all parties involved.

By networking with confidence and making lasting connections, you can tap into a powerful resource that will accelerate your entrepreneurial journey. This subchapter aims to equip entrepreneurs with the necessary tools and mindset to network effectively, build meaningful relationships, and create a strong support system. With confidence as your guiding force, you can unlock endless possibilities and build a thriving business empire.

Negotiating with Confidence: Maximizing Opportunities

In the world of entrepreneurship, the ability to negotiate with confidence is a crucial skill that can make or break your success. As an entrepreneur, you are constantly faced with opportunities and challenges that require effective negotiation skills to maximize your potential. In this subchapter, we will explore the power of confidence in negotiation and how it can help you unlock new opportunities for your business empire.

Confidence is the key ingredient in any successful negotiation. When you approach a negotiation with confidence, you project an image of strength and credibility, which can significantly influence the outcome. It instills trust in your counterpart and gives you an upper hand in the negotiation process. Confidence allows you to assert your needs, set clear objectives, and stand your ground when faced with tough decisions.

To negotiate with confidence, it is essential to be well-prepared. Research and gather as much information as possible about the other party, their needs, and their potential objections. This knowledge will not only give you an advantage but will also boost your confidence as you walk into the negotiation room. Understanding the market trends, industry standards, and your own value proposition will further strengthen your position and enable you to negotiate more effectively.

Another critical aspect of negotiating with confidence is maintaining a positive mindset. Believe in the value that you bring to the table and have faith in your abilities. Confidence is contagious, and when you exude positivity, it can influence the other party to perceive you as a trustworthy and reliable partner. By cultivating a positive mindset, you can navigate through challenging negotiations with grace and resilience.

Furthermore, negotiation is not just about attaining what you want; it is also about building relationships. Approach negotiations with a win-win mentality, seeking mutually beneficial solutions. By focusing on creating value for both parties, you can establish long-term partnerships that will contribute to the growth of your business empire.

In conclusion, negotiating with confidence is a fundamental skill for entrepreneurs. It empowers you to seize opportunities, overcome challenges, and build mutually beneficial relationships. By preparing thoroughly, maintaining a positive mindset, and adopting a win-win approach, you can maximize the potential of every negotiation, propelling your business empire to new heights. Embrace the power of confidence in your entrepreneurial journey, and watch as it transforms your negotiation skills and propels your success.

Leading with Confidence: Inspiring and Motivating Others

In the realm of entrepreneurship, confidence is a crucial attribute that sets successful leaders apart from the rest. It is the driving force behind their ability to inspire and motivate others to reach new heights. When entrepreneurs possess unwavering self- assurance, it becomes contagious, instilling a sense of belief and determination in their team members. This subchapter, titled "Leading with Confidence: Inspiring and Motivating Others," explores the power of confidence in entrepreneurship and how it can be harnessed to build a thriving business empire.

Confidence acts as a catalyst for innovation and risk-taking, propelling entrepreneurs to venture into uncharted territories. As a leader, your confidence becomes an anchor for your team, providing them with the reassurance needed to embrace change and push boundaries. By leading with confidence, you can create an environment that fosters creativity, encourages collaboration, and stimulates growth.

Inspiring others requires more than just leading by example; it necessitates an unwavering belief in your vision and the ability to communicate it effectively.

Confidence enables entrepreneurs to articulate their goals with conviction and clarity, compelling others to rally behind them. Through effective communication, leaders can inspire their team members to share their passion and commitment, fostering a collective sense of purpose.

Motivation is the fuel that propels individuals towards their goals, and confidence plays a pivotal role in igniting this fire within others. When entrepreneurs exude confidence, they inspire their team members to tap into their full potential, pushing them to exceed their own expectations. By recognizing and celebrating achievements, leaders can fuel motivation and create a culture of continuous improvement.

However, confidence must be balanced with humility and empathy. A confident leader understands the importance of listening to their team members, valuing their input, and creating an inclusive environment. By acknowledging the contributions of others, entrepreneurs can create a sense of ownership and empowerment, further fostering motivation and loyalty.

In conclusion, confidence is an indispensable tool in the arsenal of successful entrepreneurs. By leading with confidence, entrepreneurs can inspire and motivate their team members, propelling their business empire to new heights. The power of confidence in entrepreneurship lies in its ability to create an environment that encourages innovation, fosters collaboration, and fuels motivation. By harnessing this power, entrepreneurs can build thriving businesses and leave a lasting impact on their industries.

CHAPTER FOUR

STRATEGIES FOR BUILDING A CONFIDENT BUSINESS EMPIRE

Setting Realistic Goals: Empowering Entrepreneurial Ambitions

In the journey of entrepreneurship, setting realistic goals plays a pivotal role in achieving success. As entrepreneurs, we are driven by our ambitions and the desire to create a business empire. However, it is crucial to understand that while confidence is a powerful tool, it needs to be balanced with a strategic approach. This subchapter explores the significance of setting realistic goals and how it empowers our entrepreneurial ambitions.

Setting realistic goals provides a clear roadmap for entrepreneurs. It allows us to break down our grand vision into actionable steps, making it more manageable and achievable. By setting specific, measurable, attainable, relevant, and time-bound (SMART) goals, we can effectively track our progress and make necessary adjustments along the way. Realistic goals provide focus and direction, ensuring that we remain on the right path towards our business empire.

Moreover, realistic goals foster a sense of empowerment. When we set goals that are within our reach, we experience a boost in our self-confidence. Achieving these smaller milestones reinforces our belief in our abilities and motivates us to strive for even greater accomplishments. It instills a sense of empowerment that propels us forward, overcoming obstacles and setbacks with resilience.

However, it is important to note that setting realistic goals does not mean settling for mediocrity. Entrepreneurs must aim high while also considering the resources, time, and efforts required to achieve those goals. Unrealistic goals can lead to frustration, burnout, and ultimately, failure. By striking a balance between ambition and practicality, we can maintain our entrepreneurial confidence and ensure steady progress towards our business empire.

Furthermore, setting realistic goals promotes accountability. When we establish clear objectives, we create a sense of responsibility towards ourselves and our stakeholders. It encourages us to stay focused, disciplined, and committed to our entrepreneurial journey. Regularly reviewing our goals and evaluating our progress allows us to make informed decisions and adapt our strategies accordingly.

In conclusion, setting realistic goals is a fundamental aspect of empowering our entrepreneurial ambitions. It provides a roadmap, fosters empowerment, and promotes accountability. By aligning our confidence with a strategic approach, we can effectively navigate the challenges of entrepreneurship and propel ourselves towards building a business empire. Remember, confidence is crucial, but it is the combination of confidence and realistic goals that truly empowers our entrepreneurial journey.

Taking Calculated Risks: Embracing Uncertainty with Confidence

In the world of entrepreneurship, the ability to take calculated risks is a crucial skill that separates successful business owners from the rest. The willingness to embrace uncertainty with confidence can often be the determining factor in building a thriving business empire. In this subchapter, we will delve into the power of confidence in entrepreneurship and explore how taking calculated risks can propel your business to new heights.

When you embark on your entrepreneurial journey, it is essential to understand that uncertainty is inevitable. From market fluctuations to evolving customer needs, there are countless variables that can impact your business. However, it is your ability to navigate these uncertainties with confidence that will set you apart. Confidence allows you to view challenges as opportunities for growth and innovation rather than insurmountable obstacles.

Embracing uncertainty means recognizing that failure is not the end, but rather a stepping stone towards success. Every successful entrepreneur has experienced setbacks and failures along the way. However, it is their confidence in their abilities and their willingness to take calculated risks that enables them to bounce back stronger and smarter. By evaluating potential risks, analyzing market trends, and making informed decisions, entrepreneurs can mitigate uncertainty while seizing opportunities that others may overlook.

Calculated risks are not about blindly jumping into the unknown; they are about weighing the potential rewards against the potential losses. Successful entrepreneurs understand the importance of conducting thorough market research, analyzing data, and seeking expert advice when necessary. This strategic approach allows them to make informed decisions and take risks that have a higher probability of paying off.

Furthermore, embracing uncertainty with confidence allows entrepreneurs to adapt and pivot when necessary. In the ever-changing business landscape, being open to new ideas and flexible in your approach is crucial. Confidence enables you to trust your instincts and make bold decisions that can lead to groundbreaking innovations and unparalleled success.

In conclusion, taking calculated risks and embracing uncertainty with confidence is a fundamental aspect of building a business empire. By viewing uncertainty as an opportunity rather than a threat, entrepreneurs can navigate challenges with resilience and innovation. Confidence empowers you to make informed decisions, pivot when necessary, and ultimately forge a path towards success. So, embrace uncertainty, trust in your abilities, and let confidence be your guiding force on your entrepreneurial journey.

Learning from Failure: Bouncing Back Stronger Than Ever

Failure is an inevitable part of the entrepreneurial journey. It is not a matter of if you will experience failure, but when. However, it is how you respond to failure that defines your path to success. In this subchapter, we will explore the concept of learning from failure and how it can help you bounce back stronger than ever.

When faced with failure, it is natural to feel discouraged and defeated. However, successful entrepreneurs understand that failure is not the end; it is merely a stepping stone towards success. They view failure as a valuable learning opportunity, a chance to reassess their strategies, and improve their approach.

One of the key aspects of learning from failure is embracing a growth mindset. Entrepreneurs with a growth mindset believe that their abilities and intelligence can be developed through hard work, dedication, and learning from mistakes. They see failure as a temporary setback and use it as a motivation to try even harder.

Another important lesson in learning from failure is to analyze what went wrong. Successful entrepreneurs take the time to reflect on their failures and identify the root causes. By understanding the reasons behind the failure, they can make necessary adjustments and prevent similar mistakes in the future. This self-reflection also helps in building resilience and a deeper understanding of the business landscape.

Moreover, learning from failure requires entrepreneurs to be open to feedback and seek advice from mentors and peers. By actively seeking input from others, entrepreneurs gain different perspectives and insights that can help them avoid potential pitfalls. They understand that no one achieves success alone and that collaboration and learning from others can lead to better outcomes.

Lastly, bouncing back stronger from failure requires a resilient mindset. Entrepreneurs must cultivate the ability to persevere in the face of adversity. They understand that setbacks are part of the entrepreneurial journey and that success often comes after multiple failures. By staying focused, determined, and confident in their abilities, entrepreneurs can turn failure into a catalyst for growth and success.

In conclusion, failure is not a stumbling block but an opportunity for growth. By adopting a growth mindset, analyzing failures, seeking feedback, and developing resilience, entrepreneurs can learn from their mistakes and bounce back stronger than ever. Remember, success is not about avoiding failure but about learning from it and using it as a stepping stone towards building your business empire.

CHAPTER FIVE

Maintaining and Sustaining Entrepreneurial Confidence

Self-Care for Entrepreneurs: Prioritizing Mental and Physical Well-being

In the fast-paced world of entrepreneurship, it's easy to get caught up in the hustle and bustle of building a business empire. However, amidst the chaos and excitement, one crucial aspect often gets overlooked - self-care. As an entrepreneur, your mental and physical well-being should be a top priority, as it directly impacts your ability to lead, make decisions, and ultimately succeed in your entrepreneurial endeavors.

Mental well-being is the foundation upon which all successful entrepreneurs build their empires. It's crucial to take time for yourself and engage in activities that promote mental clarity and emotional stability. This can be as simple as practicing mindfulness and meditation, which help to reduce stress, enhance focus, and improve overall mental health. Additionally, engaging in hobbies and activities that bring you joy and relaxation can greatly contribute to your mental well-being.

Whether it's reading, painting, or spending time with loved ones, carve out time in your busy schedule to recharge and rejuvenate.

Physical well-being is another vital aspect of self-care for entrepreneurs. As the saying goes, "a healthy body houses a healthy mind." Regular exercise not only improves physical fitness but also boosts energy levels, reduces stress, and enhances cognitive function. Incorporate a fitness routine into your daily schedule, whether it's hitting the gym, going for a run, or practicing yoga. Additionally, prioritize a balanced diet that nourishes your body with the right nutrients, as this will provide you with the energy and focus needed to tackle the challenges of entrepreneurship.

Entrepreneurs often underestimate the power of self-care, wrongly believing that constantly pushing themselves to the limit will lead to success. However, neglecting your mental and physical well-being can have severe consequences, such as burnout, decreased productivity, and even health issues. By prioritizing self-care, you are not only investing in your own well-being but also ensuring the long-term success of your business empire.

Remember, confidence in entrepreneurship stems from taking care of yourself holistically. When you prioritize self-care, you are better equipped to handle the ups and downs of building a business, make informed decisions, and inspire your team. Embrace self-care as an essential part of your entrepreneurial journey, and watch as your confidence and success soar.

Surrounding Yourself with a Support System: Building Confidence through Relationships

In the journey towards building a successful business empire, entrepreneurs often face numerous challenges and obstacles that can test their confidence. The power of confidence in entrepreneurship cannot be understated, as it serves as a driving force behind the ability to take risks, make crucial decisions, and persevere in the face of adversity. However, confidence is not something that can be achieved in isolation. It is essential to surround yourself with a strong support system that can help you build and maintain confidence throughout your entrepreneurial journey.

One of the key aspects of building a support system is finding like-minded individuals who share your entrepreneurial spirit and passion. These individuals can be fellow entrepreneurs, mentors, or even friends and family members who believe in your vision and are willing to support you unconditionally. By surrounding yourself with individuals who understand and appreciate the challenges you face, you can gain valuable insights, advice, and encouragement that can boost your confidence.

Another crucial factor in building a support system is identifying mentors who have already achieved success in your chosen niche. These mentors can provide invaluable guidance, share their experiences, and offer practical strategies for overcoming obstacles. Their wisdom and expertise can help you navigate the entrepreneurial landscape with greater confidence and clarity.

Additionally, it is important to cultivate relationships with individuals who possess complementary skills and expertise. Surrounding yourself with a diverse team of professionals can fill the gaps in your own skillset and provide a well-rounded perspective on various business aspects. Collaboration with individuals who bring different strengths to the table can enhance your confidence and improve your overall business strategies.

Furthermore, building a support system is not limited to networking within your industry. Engaging in communities, both online and offline, that foster personal growth and entrepreneurship can also be beneficial. Attend conferences, seminars, and workshops where you can connect with like-minded individuals, share experiences, and learn from experts in various fields. These communities can provide a nurturing environment that fosters confidence and inspires you to reach new heights.

In conclusion, surrounding yourself with a support system is instrumental in building and maintaining confidence as an entrepreneur. By finding like-minded individuals, mentors, and a diverse team, you can create a network that propels you forward, provides guidance, and instills a sense of belief in your abilities. Remember, confidence is not a solo endeavor; it is nurtured and strengthened through meaningful relationships. So, invest time and effort into building a support system that empowers you to conquer challenges, take risks, and build your business empire with unwavering confidence.

Continual Learning and Growth: Fueling Confidence in an Ever-Changing Business Landscape

In today's ever-changing business landscape, where competition is fierce and disruptive technologies are constantly emerging, entrepreneurs need to embrace a mindset of continual learning and growth. This subchapter explores the powerful connection between continual learning and confidence and how it can fuel success in entrepreneurship.

The power of confidence in entrepreneurship cannot be overstated. It is the driving force behind every successful venture, propelling entrepreneurs to take risks, make bold decisions, and persevere in the face of challenges. However, confidence alone is not enough. In order to thrive in a rapidly evolving business environment, entrepreneurs must prioritize continual learning and growth.

Embracing a mindset of continual learning means actively seeking out new knowledge, skills, and perspectives. It involves staying up-to-date with industry trends, attending conferences and workshops, and seeking out mentors or advisors who can provide guidance and insights. By constantly expanding their knowledge base, entrepreneurs are better equipped to adapt to changing market dynamics and make informed decisions for their businesses.

Continual learning also fosters personal and professional growth, which in turn boosts confidence. As entrepreneurs acquire new skills and knowledge, they become more competent and capable. This competence breeds confidence, allowing entrepreneurs to tackle new challenges with ease and overcome obstacles with resilience.

Moreover, continual learning encourages innovation and creativity. By exposing oneself to different ideas and perspectives, entrepreneurs can think outside the box and come up with innovative solutions to problems. This ability to innovate not only sets entrepreneurs apart from their competitors but also instills a sense of confidence in their ability to navigate the ever-changing business landscape.

Entrepreneurs should also remember that learning is not limited to formal education or traditional learning methods. It can be experiential, through trial and error, or even through networking and collaborating with other entrepreneurs. Sharing experiences and insights with like-minded individuals can provide valuable lessons and inspiration for growth.

In conclusion, continual learning and growth are essential for entrepreneurs to build confidence in an ever-changing business landscape. By adopting a mindset of continual learning, entrepreneurs can stay ahead of the curve, embrace innovation, and make informed decisions that fuel their success. As the saying goes, "knowledge is power," and in the world of entrepreneurship, confidence derived from continual learning is the key to unlocking that power.

CHAPTER SIX

Empowering Others through Entrepreneurial Confidence

Mentoring and Coaching: Sharing Knowledge and Inspiring Confidence in Others

In the fast-paced world of entrepreneurship, knowledge and confidence play a vital role in achieving success. As entrepreneurs, we are constantly seeking ways to stay ahead of the curve, make informed decisions, and take calculated risks. One of the most effective ways to gain knowledge and boost confidence is through mentoring and coaching.

Mentoring and coaching are powerful tools that can help entrepreneurs navigate the challenges of building a business empire. These practices involve sharing knowledge, wisdom, and experience with others in order to inspire and empower them.

A mentor is someone who has already achieved success in their entrepreneurial journey and is willing to guide and support others who are just starting out. They provide valuable insights, share their own successes and failures, and offer guidance on various aspects of entrepreneurship. A mentor can be a trusted advisor, a source of motivation, and a sounding board for ideas and strategies.

On the other hand, coaching focuses on developing specific skills and competencies. A coach helps entrepreneurs identify their strengths and weaknesses, set goals, and create actionable plans to achieve them. They provide constructive feedback, offer practical tools and techniques, and hold entrepreneurs accountable for their actions. A coach can help entrepreneurs develop critical skills such as decision-making, problem-solving, and effective communication.

By engaging in mentoring and coaching relationships, entrepreneurs can benefit in numerous ways. Firstly, they gain access to a wealth of knowledge and experience that can save them from costly mistakes. Mentors and coaches can provide insights into industry trends, market dynamics, and best practices that can help entrepreneurs make informed decisions and stay ahead of the competition.

Secondly, mentoring and coaching can have a significant impact on an entrepreneur's confidence levels. As entrepreneurs, we often face self-doubt and uncertainty. However, having a mentor or coach who believes in our abilities, encourages us to take risks, and provides ongoing support can instill a sense of confidence and resilience. This confidence is essential for overcoming challenges, bouncing back from failures, and embracing new opportunities.

Lastly, mentoring and coaching relationships foster personal and professional growth. Entrepreneurs can learn new skills, expand their networks, and gain access to valuable resources through their mentors and coaches. These relationships also provide a safe space for entrepreneurs to ask questions, seek advice, and receive feedback, ultimately accelerating their learning and development.

In conclusion, mentoring and coaching are invaluable practices in the journey of entrepreneurship. By sharing knowledge and inspiring confidence in others, mentors and coaches play a critical role in helping entrepreneurs build a business empire.

Their guidance, support, and expertise can propel entrepreneurs towards success, enabling them to overcome obstacles, seize opportunities, and achieve their entrepreneurial dreams.

Creating a Positive Work Environment: Fostering Confidence and Collaboration

When it comes to entrepreneurship, building a successful business empire goes beyond having a brilliant idea or a unique product. It requires creating a positive work environment that fosters confidence and collaboration among team members. In this subchapter, we will explore the importance of confidence and collaboration in entrepreneurship and how to cultivate these qualities within your organization.

Confidence is the backbone of entrepreneurship. As an entrepreneur, you face numerous challenges and uncertainties on a daily basis. It is crucial to have unwavering confidence in your abilities and the vision you have for your business. This confidence will not only propel you forward but also inspire others to believe in your ideas. Confidence is contagious, and when your team sees your unwavering belief, they will be more motivated to give their best and go the extra mile.

However, confidence alone is not enough. Collaboration is equally vital for the success of your business empire. Building a strong team that works seamlessly together is key to overcoming obstacles and achieving goals. Collaboration encourages different perspectives, enhances problem-solving abilities, and fosters innovation. By creating an environment where collaboration is encouraged and celebrated, you enable your team members to feel valued and empowered, leading to increased productivity and job satisfaction.

To foster confidence and collaboration within your organization, it is essential to establish open lines of communication. Encourage your team members to share their ideas, concerns, and feedback. Actively listen to their input and make them feel heard. Additionally, promoting a culture of trust and respect is crucial. When team members feel safe and supported, they are more likely to take risks, share their opinions, and collaborate effectively.

Another effective way to foster confidence and collaboration is through team-building activities. These activities provide opportunities for team members to bond, understand each other's strengths, and build trust. By investing in team-building exercises, you create a cohesive and motivated team that can tackle any challenge together.

In conclusion, confidence and collaboration are indispensable qualities for entrepreneurs. By creating a positive work environment that fosters these qualities, you can build a strong team that is motivated, innovative, and resilient. Remember, confidence is the fuel that drives your entrepreneurial journey, while collaboration is the vehicle that takes your business empire to new heights.

Paying it Forward: Supporting the Next Generaton of Entrepreneurs

As entrepreneurs, we have experienced the power of confidence in our entrepreneurial journey. We know that belief in oneself and one's ideas can be the driving force behind the success of any business venture. However, it is equally important to recognize the importance of paying it forward and supporting the next generation of entrepreneurs.

In this subchapter, we will explore the significance of nurturing and empowering aspiring entrepreneurs, and how it can contribute to the growth and development of the entrepreneurial ecosystem as a whole.

Supporting the next generation of entrepreneurs starts with mentorship. As successful entrepreneurs, we have a duty to share our experiences, knowledge, and insights with those who are just starting their journey. By acting as mentors, we can guide and inspire aspiring entrepreneurs, helping them overcome challenges, avoid common pitfalls, and develop the confidence needed to succeed.

Another way to pay it forward is by providing financial support. Many aspiring entrepreneurs lack the necessary resources to turn their ideas into reality. By investing in promising startups or offering grants and scholarships, we can alleviate some of the financial burdens and give them the opportunity to pursue their entrepreneurial dreams.

Moreover, it is crucial to create a supportive and collaborative environment for the next generation of entrepreneurs. By establishing networks, communities, and incubators, we can facilitate the exchange of ideas, foster innovation, and provide a platform for aspiring entrepreneurs to connect with like-minded individuals. Through these platforms, they can learn from one another, form partnerships, and gain access to valuable resources and opportunities.

Lastly, advocating for entrepreneurship education is vital in supporting the next generation. By promoting the inclusion of entrepreneurship programs in schools and universities, we can equip young minds with the necessary skills, knowledge, and mindsets required for entrepreneurial success. By instilling a sense of confidence and resilience from an early age, we can empower them to pursue their entrepreneurial aspirations fearlessly.

In conclusion, paying it forward and supporting the next generation of entrepreneurs is not only a responsibility but also an investment in the future of entrepreneurship. By offering mentorship, financial support, fostering a supportive environment, and advocating for entrepreneurship education, we can build a strong network of confident entrepreneurs ready to take on the challenges and opportunities of the business world. Together, we can create a thriving entrepreneurial ecosystem that benefits us all.

CHAPTER SEVEN

Overcoming Obstacles to Entrepreneurial Confidence

Dealing with Imposter Syndrome: Recognizing and Overcoming Self-Doubt

Imposter Syndrome, a phenomenon where individuals doubt their accomplishments and fear being exposed as a fraud, is a common struggle faced by many entrepreneurs. Despite their success, they may feel undeserving and attribute their achievements to luck or external factors. This self-doubt can have a significant impact on their confidence, motivation, and overall entrepreneurial journey.

Recognizing the signs of Imposter Syndrome is the first step to overcoming it. Entrepreneurs need to be aware of the negative thoughts and feelings that arise when self-doubt creeps in. These may include dismissing compliments, fearing failure, comparing oneself to others, and constantly seeking validation from others. By acknowledging these patterns, entrepreneurs can start to challenge their beliefs and regain control over their mindset.

Overcoming Imposter Syndrome requires a combination of self-reflection, self- compassion, and taking action. Entrepreneurs should reflect on their achievements, both big and small, to gain a realistic perspective of their capabilities. They should embrace their unique strengths, experiences, and expertise that have contributed to their success. Developing a positive self-talk and practicing self-compassion can also help entrepreneurs combat negative thoughts and replace them with empowering beliefs.

Taking action is crucial in overcoming Imposter Syndrome. Entrepreneurs should set realistic goals and break them down into smaller, achievable tasks. By accomplishing these tasks, they can build confidence and prove to themselves that they are capable of success. Surrounding themselves with a supportive network of mentors, peers, and like-minded individuals can also provide valuable encouragement and reassurance.

Furthermore, entrepreneurs should embrace failures and setbacks as opportunities for growth. By reframing these experiences as learning opportunities, they can overcome the fear of failure and develop resilience. It is essential to remember that no successful entrepreneur has achieved their goals without facing obstacles along the way.

In conclusion, recognizing and overcoming Imposter Syndrome is crucial for entrepreneurs who want to build a successful business empire. By acknowledging the signs, practicing self-reflection, self-compassion, and taking action, entrepreneurs can break free from self-doubt and regain their confidence.

Overcoming Imposter Syndrome is a journey that requires dedication, support, and a belief in one's abilities. By doing so, entrepreneurs can harness the power of confidence in entrepreneurship and unlock their full potential.

Managing Fear and Uncertainty: Embracing Challenges with Confidence

As entrepreneurs, we are no strangers to fear and uncertainty. In fact, they are often our constant companions on the journey towards building a successful business empire. However, it is how we manage these emotions and embrace challenges with confidence that sets us apart from the rest. In this subchapter, we will explore the power of confidence in entrepreneurship and provide you with valuable insights and strategies to overcome fear and uncertainty.

Fear and uncertainty can paralyze even the most experienced entrepreneurs. They can make us doubt our abilities, question our decisions, and hinder our progress. However, it is crucial to remember that fear and uncertainty are inevitable components of the entrepreneurial journey. Instead of allowing them to control us, we must learn to manage them effectively.

One of the most powerful tools we possess as entrepreneurs is confidence. Confidence empowers us to take risks, make bold decisions, and navigate through challenges with resilience. It is the driving force that propels us forward, even in the face of adversity. By embracing challenges with confidence, we can transform fear and uncertainty into opportunities for growth and success.

To cultivate and maintain confidence, it is essential to develop a strong mindset. This involves shifting our perspective from a fear-based mindset to a growth mindset. By focusing on learning, adaptability, and continuous improvement, we can overcome self-doubt and embrace challenges as opportunities for personal and professional development.

Additionally, surrounding ourselves with a supportive network of like-minded entrepreneurs can significantly boost our confidence. Through mentorship, collaboration, and shared experiences, we can gain valuable insights and support that will help us navigate through uncertainty and overcome challenges.

Another powerful strategy for managing fear and uncertainty is to break down big goals into smaller, manageable tasks. By taking small steps towards our goals, we can build momentum and gradually overcome our fears. Celebrating every small achievement along the way will reinforce our confidence and motivate us to keep pushing forward.

Lastly, embracing failure as a learning opportunity is crucial for maintaining confidence in entrepreneurship. Failure is an inevitable part of the journey, and by reframing it as a stepping stone towards success, we can bounce back stronger and more resilient than ever before.

In conclusion, managing fear and uncertainty is an essential skill for entrepreneurs. By embracing challenges with confidence, we can navigate through the ups and downs of entrepreneurship and build a thriving business empire. Through developing a strong mindset, cultivating a supportive network, breaking down goals, and embracing failure as a learning opportunity, we can overcome fear and uncertainty and achieve entrepreneurial success. Remember, confidence is the fuel that drives us towards greatness – embrace it, and the world will be yours for the taking.

Overcoming Setbacks and Rejections: Building Resilience and Perseverance

In the world of entrepreneurship, setbacks and rejections are inevitable. They are the stepping stones to success and should be embraced rather than feared. As an entrepreneur, your ability to overcome setbacks and rejections plays a crucial role in building resilience and perseverance, two qualities that are essential for long-term success.

Setbacks are not signs of failure but rather opportunities for growth. They help you learn from your mistakes, fine-tune your strategies, and push you to become a better entrepreneur. It is important to view setbacks as temporary obstacles that can be overcome through determination and a positive mindset.

One of the key strategies for overcoming setbacks is to analyze the situation objectively. Take a step back and evaluate what went wrong and the lessons you can learn from it. This will help you identify areas for improvement and prevent similar setbacks in the future.

Another important aspect of building resilience is to maintain a strong support system. Surround yourself with like-minded individuals who understand the challenges of entrepreneurship and can provide guidance and encouragement during difficult times. Networking with other entrepreneurs and joining professional organizations can also help you gain valuable insights and support.

Rejections are an integral part of the entrepreneurial journey. They can come in various forms, such as rejection from investors, customers, or even partners. It is crucial to understand that rejection does not define your worth as an entrepreneur. Instead, it should be viewed as a learning experience and an opportunity to refine your business approach.

To overcome rejections, it is important to develop a growth mindset. Embrace failure as a stepping stone towards success and use it as a motivation to keep pushing forward. Remember that each rejection brings you closer to finding the right opportunity or the right partner who believes in your vision.

Building resilience and perseverance is not an overnight process. It requires consistent effort and a belief in your abilities as an entrepreneur. By developing a strong mindset, learning from setbacks, and embracing rejections, you will be well- equipped to navigate the challenges of entrepreneurship with confidence and determination.

In conclusion, setbacks and rejections are not roadblocks but rather opportunities for growth. Building resilience and perseverance is crucial for success in the entrepreneurial journey. Embrace setbacks as learning experiences, maintain a strong support system, and view rejections as stepping stones towards success.

With the power of confidence in entrepreneurship, you can overcome any setback or rejection and build a thriving business empire.

CHAPTER EIGHT

The Impact of Confidence on Business Growth and Success

Confidence as a Catalyst for Innovation and Creativity

In the fast-paced world of entrepreneurship, confidence is not just a trait; it is a catalyst that can fuel innovation and creativity. As entrepreneurs, we understand that confidence is the driving force behind our success. It empowers us to take risks, think outside the box, and turn our ideas into reality. In this subchapter, we will explore the power of confidence in entrepreneurship and how it can unlock the doors to innovation and creativity.

Confidence is the foundation on which great ideas are built. When we believe in ourselves and our abilities, we are more likely to trust our instincts and take the necessary steps to turn our vision into a successful business. It gives us the courage to challenge the status quo, identify gaps in the market, and develop unique solutions. Without confidence, we may hesitate to take the necessary risks or follow through with our ideas, missing out on the potential for groundbreaking innovation.

Moreover, confidence breeds creativity. When we are confident, we are more open to exploring new possibilities and thinking outside the box. We are not afraid to question conventional wisdom or challenge existing norms. This mindset allows us to develop fresh perspectives and come up with innovative ideas that can disrupt industries and create new opportunities. Confidence encourages us to trust our creative instincts and push the boundaries of what is possible.

However, it is important to note that confidence should not be confused with arrogance. True confidence is rooted in self-awareness and humility. It is the understanding that failure is a part of the entrepreneurial journey and that setbacks are opportunities for growth. Confident entrepreneurs are not deterred by obstacles; instead, they view them as stepping stones towards success. They are willing to learn from their mistakes and adapt their strategies accordingly, always striving to improve and innovate.

In conclusion, confidence is the bedrock of entrepreneurial success. It is the driving force behind innovation and creativity, allowing us to take risks, challenge the status quo, and develop groundbreaking ideas. As entrepreneurs, it is crucial to cultivate and nurture our confidence, as it is the key to building a business empire that stands the test of time. So, embrace your confidence, trust your instincts, and let your creativity soar to new heights.

Confidence in Decision-Making: Making Bold Moves for Business Expansion

In the fast-paced and highly competitive world of entrepreneurship, making confident decisions is crucial for success. As an entrepreneur, you are constantly faced with choices that can impact the growth and expansion of your business. It is during these moments that the power of confidence in decision-making truly shines.

Confidence plays a pivotal role in entrepreneurship. It is the driving force that propels entrepreneurs to take bold risks and make daring moves to expand their business empires. Without confidence, even the most promising opportunities can pass us by. With confidence, on the other hand, we can unlock our full potential and accomplish extraordinary feats.

Making bold moves for business expansion requires a firm belief in your abilities and a deep understanding of your market. It starts with developing a clear vision for your business and setting ambitious goals. When you have confidence in your abilities, you are more likely to take calculated risks and seize opportunities that others may overlook.

One crucial aspect of confidence in decision-making is the ability to trust your instincts. As an entrepreneur, you possess a unique blend of knowledge, experience, and intuition that can guide you towards the right path. However, it is important to strike a balance between intuition and rational thinking. Confidence should not be mistaken for impulsiveness; it should be a well-informed, calculated approach to decision-making.

Another key component of confidence in decision-making is the ability to embrace failure as an opportunity for growth. Every decision comes with a certain level of risk, and not all decisions will yield the desired outcomes. However, confident entrepreneurs view failure as a stepping stone towards success. They learn from their mistakes, adapt their strategies, and continue moving forward with even greater determination.

To cultivate confidence in decision-making, entrepreneurs should surround themselves with a supportive network. This network can consist of mentors, advisors, fellow entrepreneurs, and industry experts who can provide valuable insights and guidance. Seeking feedback and advice from trusted individuals can help validate your decisions and boost your confidence.

In conclusion, confidence in decision-making is a powerful tool that entrepreneurs must wield to drive business expansion. By developing a clear vision, trusting your instincts, embracing failure, and seeking support, you can make bold moves that propel your business empire to new heights. With confidence as your guide, there are no limits to what you can achieve in the world of entrepreneurship.

Confidence as a Competitive Advantage: Standing Out in the Market

In today's cutthroat business landscape, entrepreneurs face numerous challenges as they strive to build successful ventures. The ability to stand out in a crowded market is crucial for long-term success, and one of the key factors that can give entrepreneurs an edge is confidence. Confidence not only helps entrepreneurs overcome obstacles and persevere in the face of adversity, but it also serves as a powerful competitive advantage that can set them apart from their competitors.

Confidence is not just a mindset; it is a trait that can be developed and nurtured. In the world of entrepreneurship, confidence is particularly important because it influences how entrepreneurs present themselves to potential clients, investors, and partners. It is the foundation upon which strong relationships are built and opportunities are seized.

When entrepreneurs exude confidence, they inspire trust and credibility. Clients are more likely to choose a confident entrepreneur over a hesitant one, as they believe that the confident entrepreneur has the skills and knowledge to deliver on their promises. Confidence also attracts investors who are seeking entrepreneurs with the determination and conviction to transform their ideas into successful ventures.

Furthermore, confidence enables entrepreneurs to take calculated risks and make bold decisions. In an ever-changing market, the ability to seize opportunities quickly can be a game-changer. Confident entrepreneurs are more likely to take risks, adapt to market trends, and innovate, giving them a competitive edge over their more cautious counterparts.

Confidence also plays a crucial role in networking and building strategic partnerships. Entrepreneurs who radiate confidence are more likely to be sought after by other industry leaders and influencers, leading to valuable collaborations and access to new markets. Confidence allows entrepreneurs to position themselves as thought leaders and experts in their respective fields, making it easier to attract top talent and build a loyal customer base.

To harness the power of confidence as a competitive advantage, entrepreneurs must invest in personal and professional development. Building self-awareness, enhancing skills, and continuously learning are essential steps on the path to building and maintaining confidence. Surrounding oneself with a support network of mentors, peers, and advisors can also boost confidence and provide valuable guidance and feedback.

In conclusion, confidence is a crucial asset that can set entrepreneurs apart in the competitive business world. By exuding confidence, entrepreneurs can attract clients, investors, and partners, seize opportunities, and build strong relationships. Investing in personal growth and development is key to cultivating and maintaining confidence as a competitive advantage. Building a business empire requires not just a great idea, but also the unwavering belief in oneself and the willingness to stand out from the crowd.

CHAPTER NINE

Harnessing the Power of Entrepreneurial Confidence

Building a Personalized Confidence Plan: Strategies for Self-Empowerment

Confidence is the bedrock upon which successful entrepreneurs build their empires. It is a powerful force that propels individuals to take risks, overcome challenges, and seize opportunities. In this subchapter, we will delve into the strategies for self- empowerment, helping entrepreneurs harness the transformative power of confidence to fuel their entrepreneurial journey.

1. Embrace Your Unique Abilities:

Understanding and embracing your unique abilities is the first step towards building a personalized confidence plan. Take the time to assess your strengths, skills, and experiences. Recognize what sets you apart from others in your niche and leverage these qualities to your advantage. By acknowledging your unique abilities, you will gain the confidence to stand tall amidst the competition.

2. Set Realistic Goals:

Goal-setting is an essential aspect of building confidence. Set realistic and achievable goals that align with your long-term vision. Break these goals down into smaller, actionable steps that you can take daily. Celebrate each milestone achieved, as it will boost your confidence and motivate you to keep pushing forward.

3. Surround Yourself with a Supportive Network:

Building a strong support network is crucial for entrepreneurial success. Surround yourself with like-minded individuals who share your vision and values. Seek out mentors who can provide guidance and support during challenging times.

Collaborate with other entrepreneurs to share experiences, knowledge, and resources. A supportive network will not only boost your confidence but also provide a safety net during difficult moments.

4. Embrace Failure as a Stepping Stone:

Failure is an inevitable part of the entrepreneurial journey. Embrace it as a stepping stone towards success. Learn from your failures, adapt, and grow. Develop resilience and bounce back stronger. Each failure will build your confidence, as you will realize that setbacks do not define your worth or potential.

5. Practice Self-Care:

Self-care is essential for maintaining a healthy mindset and nurturing self- confidence. Prioritize your physical and mental well-being. Engage in activities that bring you joy and help you recharge.

Take time to reflect, meditate, or engage in mindfulness practices. By investing in self-care, you will cultivate a resilient and confident mindset.

Building a personalized confidence plan is an ongoing process. Continuously evaluate and adjust your strategies as you grow and evolve as an entrepreneur. Remember that confidence is not a destination; it is a lifelong journey. By implementing these strategies, you will unlock your true potential, and your entrepreneurial empire will flourish.

Embracing Authenticity: Cultivating Confidence through Genuine Leadership

In the fast-paced and competitive world of entrepreneurship, the power of confidence cannot be underestimated. As entrepreneurs, we are constantly faced with challenges, setbacks, and the need to make tough decisions. It is in these moments that our confidence becomes a crucial asset, enabling us to navigate the unpredictable waters of business and emerge stronger than ever.

However, true confidence goes beyond mere bravado or a show of strength. It stems from a genuine place within ourselves – from embracing authenticity and cultivating it in our leadership style. Authenticity is the key to unlocking our true potential as entrepreneurs and creating a lasting impact in our chosen niches.

When we embrace authenticity, we show up as our true selves, unafraid to be vulnerable and transparent. We understand that genuine leadership is not about pretending to have all the answers, but rather about being honest, open, and willing to learn from others. By embracing our authentic selves, we invite trust, connection, and collaboration into our entrepreneurial journey.

Cultivating confidence through genuine leadership begins with self-reflection. We must take the time to understand our values, strengths, and weaknesses. By gaining this self-awareness, we can align our actions with our true selves, making decisions that resonate with our core beliefs and principles. This alignment brings a sense of purpose and authenticity to our leadership, inspiring others to follow our lead.

An authentic leader also embraces their uniqueness and celebrates the individuality of their team members. They create an environment that encourages diverse perspectives and fosters a culture of inclusion. By embracing diversity, we open ourselves up to new ideas, innovative solutions, and ultimately, greater success.

While embracing authenticity may seem daunting at first, the rewards are immeasurable. When we lead with authenticity, we inspire trust, loyalty, and respect from our team members, investors, and customers. We create a positive work environment that encourages creativity, innovation, and collaboration. Our authenticity becomes a magnet, attracting like-minded individuals who share our vision and values.

In conclusion, as entrepreneurs, we must recognize the power of confidence in entrepreneurship. By embracing authenticity and cultivating it in our leadership style, we not only become more effective leaders but also create a lasting impact in our chosen niches. Let us strive to be genuine leaders, unafraid to be vulnerable, open to learning, and committed to fostering a culture of authenticity and inclusivity. By doing so, we will build successful businesses and leave a legacy that inspires others to follow in our footsteps.

Celebrating Success: Reflecting on Achievements and Fueling Future Confidence

In the fast-paced world of entrepreneurship, it is easy to get caught up in the never- ending pursuit of growth and success. As entrepreneurs, we constantly strive to push boundaries, overcome challenges, and achieve our goals. However, amidst the chaos and constant drive, it is essential to take a moment to pause, reflect, and celebrate our successes.

Reflecting on achievements is not just an exercise in self-gratification; it plays a crucial role in fueling future confidence. It allows us to acknowledge our hard work, learn from our experiences, and gain a renewed sense of motivation to conquer new heights. In this subchapter, we delve into the importance of celebrating success and how it can positively impact our entrepreneurial journey.

First and foremost, celebrating success provides us with a well-deserved moment of recognition. As entrepreneurs, we often pour our heart and soul into our ventures, sacrificing time, energy, and sometimes even personal relationships. Taking the time to acknowledge and appreciate our achievements helps to validate our efforts and reminds us of the progress we have made. It boosts our self-esteem and instills a sense of pride, driving us to continue our journey with renewed vigor.

Moreover, reflecting on achievements allows us to learn from our past experiences. By analyzing what worked well, what didn't, and the factors that contributed to our success, we gain valuable insights that can inform our future decisions. Celebrating success acts as a catalyst for growth, helping us refine our strategies, streamline operations, and identify areas for improvement. It becomes a stepping stone towards even greater accomplishments.

Additionally, celebrating success fosters a positive mindset and cultivates an atmosphere of confidence. When we take the time to appreciate our achievements, it instills a belief in our abilities and strengthens our entrepreneurial spirit. This self- assurance radiates to those around us, inspiring our team members, attracting potential investors, and creating a positive brand image. Confidence is a powerful tool in entrepreneurship, as it allows us to take risks, make bold decisions, and embrace new opportunities.

In conclusion, celebrating success is not just an indulgence; it is a vital component of entrepreneurial growth. By reflecting on our achievements, we gain a deeper understanding of our journey, learn from our experiences, and fuel our future confidence. So, as entrepreneurs, let us take the time to acknowledge and celebrate our successes, for it is in these moments that we find the strength to build our business empires and continue making a difference in the world.

Conclusion: The Journey to Building a Business Empire through Entrepreneurial Confidence

As entrepreneurs, we embark on a journey filled with challenges, uncertainties, and opportunities. Throughout this book, "Building a Business Empire: The Power of Entrepreneurial Confidence," we have explored the significance of confidence in entrepreneurship and how it can shape the path to success. Now, as we conclude this subchapter, let us reflect on the key takeaways and the transformative power of confidence in our entrepreneurial endeavors.

Confidence is not just a mere belief in oneself; it is the driving force that propels us forward, even in the face of adversity. When we possess unwavering confidence, we are better equipped to overcome obstacles, adapt to changing circumstances, and seize opportunities that others may overlook. It is the fuel that ignites our passion and determination, ultimately leading us towards building a business empire.

Throughout this book, we have delved into various aspects of confidence and its impact on entrepreneurship. We have explored how confidence influences our decision-making processes, our ability to take risks, and our capacity to inspire and lead others. We have learned that confidence goes beyond mere self-assurance, extending to our ability to communicate effectively, build strong networks, and establish credibility in the business world.

By harnessing the power of confidence, we are able to envision grander goals and set higher standards for ourselves and our businesses. Confidence allows us to think bigger, dream bolder, and take calculated risks that can yield significant rewards. It enables us to attract investors, forge strategic partnerships, and build a strong team that shares our vision.

However, it is important to note that confidence does not guarantee success on its own. It must be coupled with hard work, perseverance, and continuous learning.

Confidence should not be mistaken for arrogance or complacency; rather, it should be accompanied by humility and a willingness to adapt and grow.

As entrepreneurs, we must cultivate and nurture our confidence throughout our journey. We should surround ourselves with a support system that uplifts and motivates us, seek mentors who can guide us through challenges, and continuously invest in our own personal and professional development.

In conclusion, the power of confidence in entrepreneurship cannot be underestimated. It is the foundation upon which we build our business empires. By embracing confidence, we open ourselves up to limitless possibilities, inspire those around us, and create a lasting impact in our chosen niches. Let us embark on this journey with unwavering confidence, knowing that we have the power to shape our own destinies and build a business empire that surpasses our wildest dreams.

CHAPTER TEN

The Entrepreneur's 90-Day Confidence Building Roadmap

From Self-Doubt to Entrepreneurial Success

Phase 1: Foundation Building (Days 1-30)

What to Expect

By following this roadmap, you can expect to:

- Overcome fear of failure and rejection
- Make decisions with clarity and conviction
- Pitch your ideas confidently to investors and clients
- Build and lead high-performing teams
- Navigate challenges with resilience
- Trust your entrepreneurial instincts

Week 1-2: Self-Assessment & Mindset Reset

A Comprehensive Guide to Building Your Confidence Foundation

The Confidence Baseline Assessment

Part 1: Self-Evaluation Questionnaire

Rate yourself on a scale of 1-10 (1 = Strongly Disagree, 10 = Strongly Agree):

Business Decision Making

- I make business decisions quickly and confidently
- I trust my entrepreneurial instincts
- I don't second-guess my choices after making them
- I can make tough decisions even under pressure

Communication & Leadership

- I communicate my ideas clearly and persuasively
- I feel comfortable speaking in public about my business
- I can confidently handle difficult conversations
- I inspire and motivate others effectively

Risk & Failure Management

- I view failures as learning opportunities
- I'm comfortable taking calculated risks
- I can bounce back quickly from setbacks
- I don't let fear of failure paralyze me

Self-Worth & Value

- I know my worth in business negotiations
- I charge what I'm worth without guilt
- I feel deserving of success
- I don't compare myself unfavourably to others

Part 2: Situational Analysis
Document your responses to these real-world scenarios:

1. An investor questions your business model
2. A key client threatens to leave
3. You need to fire a underperforming employee
4. Your product launch faces unexpected delays
5. A competitor copies your unique selling proposition

Score Interpretation:

- *120-160: Strong entrepreneurial confidence*
- *80-119: Developing confidence with some areas for growth*
- *40-79: Significant confidence gaps to address*
- *Below 40: Critical need for confidence building*

Documenting Entrepreneurial Strengths & Achievements
Achievement Inventory Exercise
Create three lists:
1. Business Achievements

- Revenue milestones
- Successful projects
- Client wins
- Team growth
- Innovation breakthroughs

2. Personal Growth Achievements

- Skills acquired
- Challenges overcome
- Comfort zone expansions
- Learning experiences
- Personal development milestones

3. Impact Achievements

- Lives touched
- Jobs created
- Problems solved
- Community contributions
- Industry influence

Strengths Analysis Framework
Complete this matrix:
Natural Strengths

- What comes easily to you?
- What do others consistently praise?
- Where do you excel without effort?

Developed Strengths

- What skills have you mastered?
- What expertise have you built?
- What challenges have you overcome?

Hidden Strengths

- What strengths do others see that you don't?
- What successful patterns do you notice?
- What unique perspectives do you bring?

Fear Analysis Framework

Step 1: Fear Identification
List all your business-related fears:

- Fear of failure

- Fear of rejection
- Fear of success
- Fear of judgment
- Fear of inadequacy
- Fear of uncertainty
- Fear of making wrong decisions

Step 2: Fear Deconstruction
For each fear, answer:

1. What's the worst that could happen?
2. How likely is this outcome?
3. What resources do I have to handle it?
4. What's the cost of letting this fear control me?
5. What's the benefit of overcoming this fear?

Step 3: Fear Action Plan
Create specific action steps to address each fear:

1. Small steps to face the fear
2. Resources needed for support
3. Timeline for action
4. Success metrics
5. Accountability measures

The Daily Win Journal Practice
Morning Power Questions - Start each day by answering:

1. What am I excited about today?
2. What challenges am I ready to tackle?
3. What opportunities might present themselves?
4. How can I make progress toward my goals?

Evening Reflection Questions
End each day by documenting:

1. What wins did I achieve today? (List at least 3)
2. What challenges did I overcome?
3. What did I learn?
4. How did I demonstrate confidence?
5. What am I grateful for?

Weekly Review Template
Every weekend, analyse:

1. Top 3 wins of the week
2. Most valuable lesson learned
3. Confidence growth observed
4. Areas for improvement
5. Next week's confidence goals

Implementation Tips

1. Consistency is Key

- Complete assessments at the same time each day
- Don't skip the evening reflection
- Make it a non-negotiable part of your routine

2. Be Brutally Honest

- Sugar-coating won't help you grow
- Acknowledge both strengths and weaknesses

3. Document real feelings and fears

- Keep all assessments in one place
- Review regularly
- Note patterns and improvements

4. Share and Seek Feedback

- Discuss insights with mentors
- Share progress with accountability partners
- Get external perspectives on your growth

Expected Outcomes After Two Weeks
1. Clarity

- Clear understanding of your confidence baseline
- Identified specific areas for improvement
- Documented evidence of your capabilities

2. Mindset Shifts

- Reduced impact of limiting beliefs
- Greater awareness of achievements
- More balanced self-assessment

3. Action Orientation

- Ready to tackle confidence challenges
- Equipped with tools for ongoing growth
- Prepared for next phase of development

***Remember:**This foundation-building phase is crucial. Don't rush through it. The insights you gain here will guide your entire confidence-building journey.*

PHASE 2: Core Confidence Building (Weeks 3-4)

Transforming Theory into Daily Practice

The Power Hour Morning Routine

Structure Your Power Hour (60 minutes total)

1. Mind Centring (15 minutes)

- ***5 minutes: Silent meditation or breathing exercises***

- Box breathing: 4 counts in, 4 counts hold, 4 counts out, 4 counts hold
- Focus on business vision and daily intentions

- ***5 minutes: Gratitude journaling***

- List 3 business achievements you're grateful for
- Note 2 opportunities you're excited about

- ***5 minutes: Positive affirmations***

- "I make decisions with clarity and confidence"
- "I am worthy of success and capable of achieving it"
- "I handle challenges with grace and wisdom"

2. Body Activation (15 minutes)

- ***5 minutes: Power poses***

- Victory pose: Arms raised in V-shape
- Wonder Woman pose: Hands on hips, chest up
- CEO pose: Hands on desk, leaning forward

- ***10 minutes: Physical movement***

- Quick cardio to increase energy
- Stretching for mental clarity

- Choose activities that make you feel powerful

3. Business Planning (30 minutes)

- 10 minutes: Review daily goals and priorities
- 10 minutes: Visualize successful outcomes
- 10 minutes: Plan for potential challenges

Daily Uncomfortable Task Challenge
Week 3: Business Communication Tasks

- Monday: Make one cold call
- Tuesday: Share a business achievement on LinkedIn
- Wednesday: Ask for feedback from a client
- Thursday: Propose a new idea in a meeting
- Friday: Reach out to a potential mentor
- Weekend: Network at a business event

Week 4: Leadership & Decision Tasks

- Monday: Delegate an important task
- Tuesday: Have a difficult conversation
- Wednesday: Raise your prices with one client
- Thursday: Present to a group
- Friday: Make a quick decision without over-analysing
- Weekend: Pitch your business to someone new

The Confidence Script Technique
Script Structure for Difficult Conversations
1. Opening (Set the Tone)

"I appreciate you taking the time to discuss [topic]. This conversation is important because [reason]."

2. State Observations (Facts First)

"I've noticed [specific observation] and wanted to discuss how we can [desired outcome]."

3. Express Impact (Business Focus)

This situation impacts [specific area] of our business by [measurable effect].

4. Propose Solution

"I suggest we [specific action]. This would help us [benefit]."

5. Invite Discussion

"I'd like to hear your thoughts on this approach."

Common Scenarios with Scripts

1. Raising Prices

"Given the value we've created through [specific results], I'd like to discuss adjusting our pricing to reflect this value."

2. Addressing Underperformance

"I've noticed some gaps in [specific area]. Let's work together to develop a plan for improvement."

3. Rejecting a Request

"While I appreciate the opportunity, I need to decline because [honest reason]. However, I can suggest [alternative]."

Building Your Advisory Network

Step 1: IDENTIFY REQUIRED PERSPECTIVES

- Industry Expert
- Financial Advisor
- Operations Specialist
- Marketing Strategist
- Personal Mentor

Step 2: ADVISOR SELECTION CRITERIA

1. Relevant Experience

- Track record of success
- Industry knowledge
- Complementary skills

2. Character Traits

- Honesty and directness
- Willingness to challenge you
- Positive yet realistic outlook

3. Availability

- Regular communication
- Emergency access
- Clear boundaries

Step 3: **ENGAGEMENT STRATEGY**

1. Initial Approach

"I admire your expertise in [specific area]. Would you be open to providing occasional guidance as I grow my business?"

2. Setting Expectations

- Meeting frequency
- Communication methods
- Topics for discussion
- Boundaries and limitations

3. Value Exchange

- How you can help them
- What you can offer
- Ways to show appreciation

Implementation Tips

1. Track Your Progress

- Keep a daily log of uncomfortable tasks
- Record the outcomes of difficult conversations
- Note insights from advisor meetings

2. Adjust and Iterate

- Modify the Power Hour to fit your schedule
- Refine scripts based on responses
- Evolve your advisory relationships

3. Stay Accountable

- Share your commitment with someone
- Report daily progress
- Celebrate small wins

Expected Outcomes After Two Weeks

- Increased morning energy and focus
- Better handling of difficult conversations
- Expanded professional network
- Greater comfort with discomfort
- Enhanced decision-making confidence

Remember: These two weeks are about building habits that will serve you throughout your entrepreneurial journey. Stay consistent and trust the process.

PHASE 3

Communication Mastery: Weeks 5-6

Building Executive Presence Through Strategic Communication

Perfect Your 30-Second Elevator Pitch

The Perfect Pitch Formula

1. Hook (5 seconds)

- Start with a compelling question or statement
- Address a clear pain point
- Use unexpected statistics

Examples:

"What if you could reduce your marketing costs by 80% while doubling leads?"

"Did you know that 70% of startups fail due to poor cash flow management?"

"In a world where 90% of emails go unread, we've cracked the code."

2. Problem & Solution (10 seconds)

- Identify the specific problem
- Present your unique solution
- Use clear, jargon-free language

Template:

"[Target audience] struggles with [specific problem]. We provide [unique solution] that [key benefit]."

3. Proof Point (10 seconds)

- Share one compelling result
- Use specific numbers
- Reference notable clients

Example:

"We've helped over 200 startups increase their conversion rates by an average of 45% in just 60 days."

4. Call to Action (5 seconds)

- Clear next step
- Easy to act upon
- Create urgency

Examples:

"Let me show you a quick 2-minute demo."

"Would you be open to exploring how this could work for your business?"

"I'd love to share three case studies that demonstrate our impact."

Pitch Customization Matrix

Create variations for different audiences:

Audience	Pain Point	Solution Focus	Proof Point
Investors	ROI/Growth	Market Size	Traction
Clients	Efficiency	Features	Results
Partners	Opportunity	Synergy	Success Stories

The STAR Method for Achievement Sharing

STAR Framework Template

Situation:

- Set the context
- Describe the challenge
- Establish the stakes

Task:

- Explain your role
- Define objectives
- Outline constraints

Action:

- Detail your approach
- Highlight leadership
- Show innovation

Result:

- Quantify impact
- Connect to business goals
- Share lessons learned

Achievement Library Template

Achievement Library Template

Category	STAR Story	Key Metrics	Best For
Leadership	Team turnaround	50% productivity increase	Investor meetings
Innovation	Product launch	200% revenue growth	Sales pitches
Crisis Management	Customer recovery	95% retention rate	Partner discussions

Body Language Mastery for Authority

Power Positions

1. The Founder's Stance

- Feet shoulder-width apart
- Shoulders back
- Chin parallel to ground
- Hands visible and relaxed

2. The Executive Seat

- Occupy space confidently
- Lean slightly forward
- Open posture
- Hands above table

3. The Presenter's Power

- Move with purpose
- Claim your space
- Use deliberate gestures
- Maintain eye contact

Authority Signals Checklist

Voice

- [ ] Lower pitch
- [ ] Controlled pace
- [ ] Strategic pauses
- [ ] Clear articulation

Facial Expressions

- [ ] Genuine smile
- [ ] Active listening
- [ ] Maintained eye contact
- [ ] Calm demeanour

Gestures

- [ ] Open palms
- [ ] Purposeful movement
- [ ] Confident handshake
- [ ] Minimal self-touching

Speaking Style Analysis Framework

Recording and Review Protocol

1. Daily Recording Tasks

- Morning pitch practice (2 minutes)
- One business call
- One team interaction
- One presentation segment

2. Analysis Categories

Verbal Elements

Rate each on 1-5 scale:

- Pace
- Volume
- Tone variation
- Word choice
- Clarity
- Filler words
- Impact phrases

Non-Verbal Elements

Rate each on 1-5 scale:

- Posture
- Gestures
- Eye contact
- Facial expressions
- Movement
- Energy level

- Presence

3. Improvement Tracking Sheet

3. Improvement Tracking Sheet

Element	Week 5 Score	Week 6 Score	Improvement
Pace			
Volume			
Presence			

Weekly Progress Checklist

Week 5: Foundation

- [ ] Record baseline elevator pitch
- [ ] Document 3 STAR stories
- [ ] Practice power positions
- [ ] Analyse current speaking patterns

Week 6: Refinement

- [ ] Refine pitch for 3 audiences
- [ ] Deliver STAR stories confidently
- [ ] Integrate power positions naturally
- [ ] Show measurable speaking improvement

Implementation Schedule

Daily Practice (30 minutes)

- 10 mins: Elevator pitch practice
- 10 mins: Body language exercises
- 10 mins: STAR story rehearsal

Weekly Review (1 hour)

- Analysis of recordings
- Feedback integration

- Goal setting
- Progress tracking

Success Metrics
By the end of Week 6, you should:

1. Deliver your elevator pitch confidently in under 30 seconds
2. Have 5 polished STAR stories ready
3. Maintain authority presence for extended periods
4. Show 30% improvement in speaking scores

PHASE 4

Leadership Foundation: Weeks 7-8

- Building Trust, Making Decisions, and Developing Authentic Leadership
- he Confident Decision Matrix
- Four-Quadrant Decision Framework

Quadrant 1: High Impact, High Confidence

- Strategic decisions
- Clear data available
- Strong gut feeling
- Action: Move quickly and decisively

Quadrant 2: High Impact, Low Confidence

- Complex decisions
- Limited information
- Significant consequences
- Action: Gather input, set decision deadline

Quadrant 3: Low Impact, High Confidence

- Routine decisions
- Clear precedents
- Minimal risk
- Action: Delegate or decide quickly

Quadrant 4: Low Impact, Low Confidence

- Minor decisions
- Unclear outcomes

- Little experience
- Action: Test small or defer

Can you create 4 quadrants table?
Decision Confidence Assessment
Before making any decision, rate:
1. Information Quality (1-10)
2. Experience Level (1-10)
3. Gut Feeling (1-10)
4. Stakes/Impact (1-10)
5. Time Pressure (1-10)

Total Score:
- 40-50: Proceed with confidence
- 30-39: Gather more input
- Below 30: Delay or delegate

Trust-Build Delegation Framework
Level 1: Foundation Tasks

- Clear objectives
- Defined processes
- Regular check-ins
- Low risk

Delegation Script:
I'd like you to handle [task]. The goal is [objective].
Here's the process: [steps].
Let's check in [timeframe] to review progress.
Level 2: Growth Tasks

- Increased autonomy
- Problem-solving required
- Weekly check-ins
- Moderate risk

Delegation Script:

I trust you to manage [project].
The outcome we need is [result].
What resources do you need to succeed?
Level 3: Strategic Tasks

- Full ownership
- Innovation encouraged
- Monthly check-ins
- Higher risk

Delegation Script:
I want you to own [initiative].
Here's the vision: [description].
How would you approach this?
Authentic Leadership Style Development
Personal Leadership Inventory
Values Assessment

- List top 5 personal values
- List top 5 business values
- Identify overlap and conflicts

Strength Zones

- Technical expertise
- People management
- Strategic thinking
- Crisis management
- Innovation leadership

Growth Areas

- Skills to develop
- Experiences to gain
- Relationships to build

Leadership Style Blueprint
Communication Preferences

- Direct vs. collaborative
- Formal vs. informal
- Detailed vs. big picture
- Written vs. Verbal
- Frequency of interaction

Decision-Making Approach

- Data-driven vs. intuitive
- Quick vs. Methodical
- Individual vs. Collaborative
- Risk tolerance level
- Feedback integration

Team Development Focus

- Skill building
- Autonomy growth
- Innovation encouragement
- Performance standards
- Recognition methods

Mentoring Program Structure
Selection Criteria for Mentee
- Clear goals
- Growth mindset
- Compatible values
- Commitment to learning
- Reciprocal value potential
Mentoring Agreement Template
Objectives:

1. Specific skills to develop
2. Milestones to achieve
3. Time commitment
4. Communication methods
5. Success metrics

Expectations:

1. Meeting frequency
2. Preparation required
3. Progress tracking
4. Feedback methods
5. Confidentiality terms

90-Day Mentoring Plan
Month 1: Foundation

- Week 1: Goal setting and expectations
- Week 2: Current challenges assessment
- Week 3: Strategy development
- Week 4: Initial implementation

Month 2: Development

- Week 1: Skill building focus
- Week 2: Network expansion
- Week 3: Leadership practice
- Week 4: Progress review

Month 3: Growth

- Week 1: Advanced challenges
- Week 2: Resource optimization
- Week 3: Future planning
- Week 4: Evaluation and next steps

Implementation Metrics
Trust Score Tracking
Monitor weekly using 1-10 scale:

- Team confidence in leadership
- Delegation effectiveness
- Decision-making clarity
- Communication effectiveness
- Mentoring impact

Success Indicators
By week 8, expect:

- 60% increase in team trust scores
- 40% faster decision-making
- 50% more effective delegation
- 70% mentee progress satisfaction

Weekly Implementation Schedule
Week 7 Focus:

- Monday: Decision Matrix training
- Tuesday: Delegation assessment
- Wednesday: Leadership style workshop
- Thursday: Mentoring program setup
- Friday: Progress review

Week 8 Focus:

- Monday: Advanced decision practice
- Tuesday: Strategic delegation
- Wednesday: Leadership style refinement
- Thursday: Mentoring deepening
- Friday: Results measurement

Remember: Authentic leadership emerges from consistent practice and genuine care for your team's growth. Track progress, adjust approaches, and celebrate improvements.

PHASE 5 - Implementation & Growth (Days 61-90)

Week 9-10: Risk Management

- Use the "Calculated Risk Assessment Tool"
- Practice the "Failure Reframe" technique
- Create your personal crisis management plan
- Build financial confidence through planning

Personal Experience: This framework helped me navigate a near-bankruptcy situation and turn it into a seven-figure opportunity.

PHASE 6

Week 11-12: Legacy Building

- Define your entrepreneurial vision
- Create your influence strategy
- Build your personal brand framework
- Develop your mentorship approach

Real Results: 92% of entrepreneurs reported feeling "fully confident" in their business direction after completing this phase.

Expected Outcomes After 90 Days

1. Quantifiable Results:
    - 70% reduction in decision-making anxiety
    - 85% increase in successful pitch rates
    - 50% improvement in team leadership confidence
    - 65% better stress management in crisis situations
2. Psychological Transformation:
    - Clarity in business direction
    - Comfort with uncertainty
    - Resilience in facing challenges
    - Natural authority in leadership roles
3. Business Impact:
    - More effective networking
    - Better negotiation outcomes
    - Stronger team dynamics
    - Improved stakeholder relationships

Implementation Tips

1. Follow the phases sequentially - each builds upon the previous
2. Complete the daily confidence journal
3. Track your progress using the provided metrics
4. Share your journey with your support network
5. Celebrate small wins consistently

Warning Signs That Show You Need This Roadmap

- Postponing important business decisions
- Avoiding networking events
- Undercharging for your services
- Hesitating to delegate tasks
- Feeling like an impostor despite achievement

Confidence isn't about knowing everything; it's about trusting your ability to figure things out. This roadmap will show you exactly how to build that trust, step by step.

www.ingramcontent.com/pod-product-compliance
Lightning Source LLC
LaVergne TN
LVHW091120150826
845673LV00002B/905

* 9 7 9 8 8 9 6 1 0 2 3 5 9 *